MW01633883

Fairest Lady

Hail Holy Queen
in Sacred Art for Young Children

BY KERRI AND KENNETH DAVISON
ART DIRECTOR RONALD LAWSON

HOLY HEROES BOOKS

HolyHeroes.com

Dedicated with gratitude
to parents and grandparents
who pass on the deep wisdom of the Faith
by reading to little children.

Note: We capitalize divine pronouns (those referring to God)
throughout our text, both for reverence and clarity.

A Note to Readers

The *Hail Holy Queen* prayer was written by a monk who lived a thousand years ago in a monastery on the island of Reichenau (in present day Germany). He was known as "Hermann the Cripple," because he was so physically disabled that he had to be carried everywhere – but all who met him admired his joyful personality and brilliant intellect.

Blessed Hermann wrote this prayer to the Blessed Virgin Mary in Latin and named it after the first line, "Salve Regina." In this book, we will help you learn the most common English translation, but we have included the original Latin text at the end of the book.

Did you know Blessed Hermann also composed a very beautiful melody for his Latin prayer? You have probably heard it, because his *Salve Regina* has become a favorite Catholic hymn throughout the world. You can listen to it being sung by my daughters at *HolyHeroes.com/HailHolyQueen*. Listen to it and follow along with the Latin words in this book until you learn it by heart!

The Queen of Heaven and Earth

When God established the Kingdom of Israel under King David, the Queen of the Kingdom was not the *wife* of the King, but rather the *mother* of the King.

When the Archangel Gabriel appeared to Mary, he revealed that her son, Jesus, would be given "the throne of His father, David… and of His Kingdom there will be no end" (Luke 1:31-33).

Mary knew this meant that as the mother of the King, she would be the Queen. And since Jesus is the King forever, ruling from Heaven, this also means she has been made by God the Queen of His Heavenly Kingdom forever.

This is why we have a prayer to the Blessed Virgin Mary called *Hail Holy Queen.*

...HOSIOR SOLE · +SVP OEM STELLA...
...CHIOR FFF...
ODITH IVEIT DVL...

Hail, Holy Queen,

"Hail" is the greeting used by the Archangel Gabriel to Mary at the Annunciation. It means "rejoice" or "be glad." "Holy" means consecrated by God, and Mary was consecrated by God in a special way: she was made free from all sin even before she was born, to make her perfect for being the mother of Jesus. Mary is the Queen of Heaven and Earth, because her Son, Jesus, is the King.

Mother
of
Mercy,

Mary is the mother of Jesus, Who is perfectly merciful because He is God.

our
life,

Every person's life on earth is a gift from God, and God gives us this earthly life through our mothers. But when Mary agreed to become the mother of Jesus, she agreed to help God give us an even more amazing life: everlasting life with Jesus in Heaven.

our
sweetness,

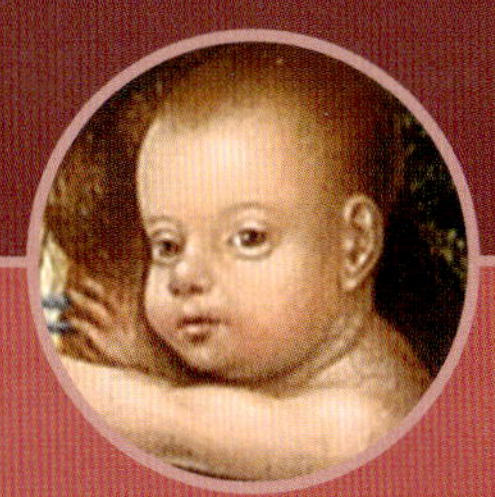

Someone who is sweet is pleasant and kind and gentle. Mary was like this to her child Jesus, just as she is to us, her spiritual children.

and
our
hope.

Even when Jesus was dying on the Cross, Mary stood beside Him

trusting in God to bring good out of such evil. We want to hope

and trust like her, so that we will someday be raised

into Heaven just as she was.

To thee
do we
cry,

We cry to Mary for help, like we cry
to our own mothers for help when we are hurt.

A dev.n de D. Ign Rosino y D. Maria Oliv

poor

banished

children

of Eve.

Adam and Eve lived in the Garden of Eden with God, but they sinned
and were sent out of the Garden (banished) to live on earth apart
from God. We are all banished children of Eve while we live here on
earth, outside of Heaven where we could live in the presence of God!   17

To thee

do we

send up

our sighs,

We are sending our sadness up to Mary and asking her for help in this life, just like we go to our own mothers on earth for comfort when we are sad.

mourning and

weeping

in this

vale of tears.

Life here on earth has sad and painful times, and we suffer because of sickness, accidents, death, our sins, and the sins of others.

AVE MARIA GRATIA PLENA
IHS XPS

Turn then, most gracious advocate,

Mary is the most gracious because she is "full of grace" as the Archangel Gabriel told her. An "advocate" is someone who asks for help on our behalf, which is what Mary does for us with her Son.

thine eyes

of mercy

toward us,

We ask that Mary look at us to see our needs.
We know she will turn to Jesus to ask that
He grant us mercy and aid.

and after

this

our exile

Our short life on earth apart from God is like being in exile
from our true home, which is with Him in Heaven forever.

show unto

us the

Blessed Fruit

of Thy Womb,

Jesus.

Babies grow inside their mothers' wombs until they are ready to be born. For this reason, we read in the Bible that Elizabeth called Jesus "the fruit of [Mary's] womb" Luke 1:42).

O clement,

Clement is another way of saying "merciful." Mary is the Mother of Mercy, because she is the Mother of Jesus.

INRI

O loving,

While Jesus was dying on the cross, He gave Mary to His Apostle, John, to be not only John's mother, but also a spiritual mother to all people. That is why Mary loves you just like your own mother does.

O sweet Virgin Mary!

Mary is the purest and sweetest of all people, except Jesus, and we are telling her how much we love and appreciate her.

℣. Pray for us,
O holy mother
of God.

Mary can pray for us to her Son, Jesus,
from her heavenly throne.

(Note: ℣ indicates that when praying with others,
this line in the prayer is spoken by the leader.)

℞. That we may be made worthy of the promises of Christ.

Jesus promised that through His Church He can make us into saints who can live with Him in Heaven for eternity.

(Note: ℞ indicates that when praying with others, this line in the prayer is spoken by everyone in response to the leader.)

Amen.

We end all our prayer with "Amen,"
which in Hebrew means "it is true."

Salve, Regína, Mater misericórdiæ,
vita, dulcédo et spes nostra, salve.
Ad te clamámus, éxsules fílii Evæ.
Ad te suspirámus geméntes et flentes
in hac lacrimárum valle.
Eia ergo, advocáta nostra,
illos tuos misericórdes óculos ad nos convérte.
Et Iesum, benedíctum fructum ventris tui,
nobis, post hoc exsílium, osténde.
O clemens, O pia, O dulcis Virgo María!

℣. Ora pro nobis, sancta Dei génetrix.
℞. Ut digni efficiámur promissiónibus Christi.

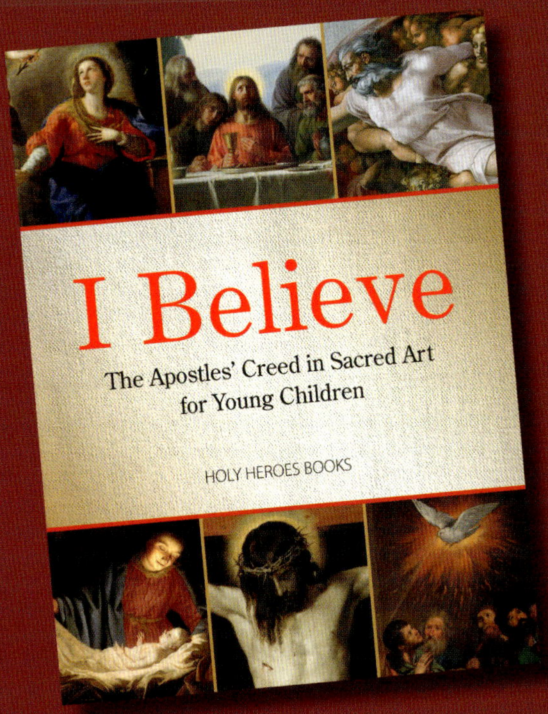

The Catechism of the Catholic Church
hails the Apostles' Creed as

"the oldest Roman catechism."

Saint Ambrose praised it as "the treasure of our soul."

Use this book as a child's introduction to this treasure,
filling young hearts and imaginations with the wonder of
our Faith through a phrase-by-phrase interpretation by the
greatest artists of Christendom!

Available at *HolyHeroes.com/SacredArt*

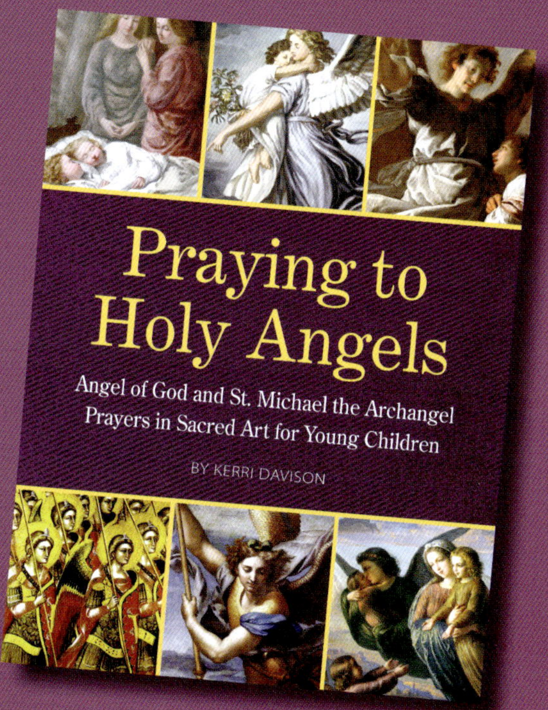

The Bible tells us about angels:

**"When the Son of Man comes in all His glory,
and all His angels with Him…"** (Matthew 25:31)

**"The whole life of the Church benefits from the mysterious
and powerful help of the angels."** (CCC 334)

In this book little children's hearts and imaginations will be
filled with what is true and beautiful about God's holy angels.
Using some of the great paintings of Christendom to illustrate
two beloved angel prayers of the Church, children will come to
know and love their own angels as true heavenly friends and
protectors.

Available at *HolyHeroes.com/SacredArt*

Painting Credits